PRECEDERE A. WILSON

Published by:
Abraham's Ink Publishing House
www.abrahamsinkph.com

ISBN:
Digital 978-1-7349236-3-6
Print 978-1-7349236-2-9

Dedication

To my children and grandchildren

Table of Contents

Forword by

Jensie J. Taylor

Purpose. What is purpose? More specifically, what is your purpose? Webster's Dictionary defines purpose as "something set up as an object or end to be attained." When God created us, He created each of us for a purpose. We all have a pivotal role to play in this world, and how will you use your gifts, talents, ideas, knowledge, and creativity to find and ignite your purpose? I remember the day I found my purpose, and since then, my life has changed for the better. Now, I am more intentional about the work I do, and I am grateful to be a source of encouragement to others. Once you find your purpose, you will be amazed at how your world opens up.

To figure out our purpose, we must continue to navigate this journey called life. Life teaches us daily about people, places, ideas, cultures, and education. The more information we learn, the greater it helps us in determining and fulfilling our purpose. Mrs. Precedere Ann Wilson, whom I endearingly refer to as "Ms. Ann," exemplified this in her new book, Legacy of Life Lessons.

Ms. Ann provides readers with lessons she has learned throughout her life. She desires to help others who are on this journey and provide them with advice and wisdom to help them avoid some of the pitfalls of life. These lessons Ms. Ann shares are part of her legacy and God's purpose for her. I hope that after reading this book, you will have a clearer understanding of the purpose God has placed on your life. Once you do, walk confidently in your purpose!

Thank you, Ms. Ann, for using your life experiences and gift of writing to assist others in navigating life and helping them find their purpose. May your lessons be invaluable to everyone who reads this book, and may you reach thousands of people with your poignant words.

Precedere A. Wilson

This book comes to you as a way for me to shine a light on my journey on this earth. I endeavor to convey a message that is clear and thought-provoking. I desire to incite growth spiritually, physically, and emotionally in the lives of those who will delve into these pages.

The content is not intended to harm anyone. Instead, it is meant to help everyone.

To my Lord and Savior: Thank You for being so patient with me as I seemingly rejected every impulse You gave me to put pen to paper. I have lived to see this day because of Your love, kindness, and mercy. You are an awesome Father.

To my husband, Elfrem: Thank you for your never-ending support and for pushing me to do anything I put my mind to. Your voice is a blanket that has kept me warm and covered in every season of life.

To my children, DeAnna and DeShaun: Thank you for being who you are and forcing me to accept it. In your own unique way, you each have brought so much joy into my life. I will forever be grateful that you call me mom. One of my greatest privileges in life has been to let you know that you are loved unconditionally, and I never want you to doubt that.

To my two wonderful, amazing, smart, talented, and lovable grandchildren and future grands: I will always light up when you walk into the room. Your presence in my life is so important. Go forth, my dear ones, and do great things. There are no limits to how far you can go. Remember the Lord in the days of your youth, and He will take you places you never dreamed of going.

Thank you to the many people who have touched my life in some way. Because of your love, laughter, rebukes, hugs, kisses, aloofness, and unwavering loyalty, I am the person I have become today.

A Note From Author's Husband

Elfrem Wilson

Ann, I applaud you for your first of many books. Legacy of Life Lessons is the first fruit of your experience on this journey of life. Your commitment and dedication to sharing your life experiences show your genuine concern for humanity. In a time in our society where things seem so unstable, I believe the people who read this book will feel and develop a sense of stability in their lives. As your husband and best friend for over 35 years, I am so godly proud of you. I love how you took that creative energy that was boiling on the inside of you and put pen to paper, and *Legacy of Life Lessons* is what was born. Thanks for your hard work and for embracing the spirit of a finisher. I believe this world has been waiting for you. I love you more!

12

A Note From Eldress

Loretta Thomas

The *Legacy of Life Lessons* is the astounding
life journey of one who is evolving
into a wonderful, marvelous, beautiful
creature, created by the hands of our
great Creator, God Almighty.

As you travel through these pages of life's lessons that reflect Precedere Wilson's legacy, I believe you will connect with her. As you approach the crossroad in your life's journey, realize you are not traveling alone. God is forever present. HE will carry you when life's turbulence comes, and it will come.

Trust in God's plan, purpose, and will for your life's pilgrimage. Every time you fall, get back up. Remember, each fall is not a failure. It is just one of life's lessons. Learn from the fall. Look up and get back up!

Precedere Wilson is a woman of God, who pursues the

heart of God. Thus, the Legacy of Life Lessons will inspire you to never stop along your journey. You will become encouraged to press forward to the finish line. We are all winners in the eyes of God Almighty, the Creator of both Heaven and Earth.

CHAPTER 1

You Were Born with Purpose

You Are Not a Mistake

The Lord shined His light on me. I was born! Oh, happy day! The thought of it brings a smile to my face…lol. I think I was born on July 22, 1969. I like to remember it as the month and year Neil Armstrong walked on the moon. The date itself holds a little bit of controversy for me. The truth is, I don't really know what day I was born.

For the first 18 years of my life, I celebrated my birthday on the 24th, until I needed a copy of my birth certificate to go into the military. That's when I discovered the actual recorded date of my birth was July 22, 1969. My mother and father both seem to agree that it was, in fact, the 24th. Who's right? Is it my parents or the mother-baby unit of Lenoir Community Hospital? Go figure! This is another story for another whole day. In this script, we will stick with the legally documented date.

To make a long story short, I am meant to be here. I am not a mistake! God intended it to be so. No matter the circumstances surrounding my getting here, I am here, and all opposing forces must deal with that. My appearance, mannerisms, and personality all encompass who I am. Some will love it, and some will detest it. Even still, I am God's creative work.

> But you are a chosen race, a royal priesthood, a holy nation. A people for his own possession, that you may proclaim the excellencies of Him who called you out of darkness into His marvelous light.
>
> *1 Peter 2:9*

Now, at 54 years old, I feel it's imperative to walk fully in this truth. You may ask, "What truth?" The truth is, I am valuable, no matter who thinks I'm not. There is intentionality in my "being." For years, I was distracted by what I thought were imperfections about me (as if God makes mistakes). I never looked at myself as anything special. As a kid my brother always made sure I was aware of what he considered my less flattering feature— my nose. Other people belittled my tiny frame (as if it were some kind of plague). My calm, unassuming personality was a wet blanket to loud, hysterical types.

If I can be candid, enduring all the external criticism damaged my self-love. As a result, I began to ask God (my Maker) what was wrong with me. I would inquire of Him as if my critics were right. Eventually, I realized if there was any error, it was in my thinking.

It was always somewhat surprising that anyone could see something good in me. I don't know why it surprised me. You would think I was born with an internal self-loathing button. Now, why wouldn't they see something good in me? After all, God created me. He formed and fashioned me. I am a rare jewel and precious to behold in the eyes of my heavenly Father, and yes, the world will notice it. They may not acknowledge it. Some will turn their heads at the brilliance of His craftsmanship, and some will be drawn to it like a magnet. Nevertheless, I am my Father's child. He made me on purpose for purpose!

Be Intentional About Your Purpose

From what I have been told, I was tiny and quiet, with a head full of hair. I was always thin, and I have been reminded of that in some form or another most of my life. To be transparent, I don't know much about my toddler life. No one ever really talked to me about those years. It is like the stories and experiences of my yesteryears are stored in a vault, somewhere without a key. Many memories are lost.

Although I don't know much about those times, one thing is certain—God had His hand on my life. He had to have been there because there is no way I would have made it this far without His guidance, love, and protection. I am a walking, talking, living, breathing miracle by my own definition. I say this because I have survived everything life has thrown my way. I have fallen many times, but God has always given me the strength to get up, like Rocky. Sometimes, I've made it on boards and broken pieces. Nevertheless, I am still here.

So, I am a miracle, and God has a purpose for my life—not just "a" purpose but a perpetual purpose. There is something that He has for me to do every minute, every day, every month, and every year of my life. This insight does not merely apply to me. It also applies to your life. It doesn't matter if you fall trying to complete your purpose. You just have to get back up. Keep it moving! Do it for yourself, but also realize that your perseverance encourages someone else. You may never know who is watching, but someone is always observing.

> Ye are our epistle written in our hearts known and read of men.
>
> *1 Corinthians 3:2*

One of my favorite motivational speakers is Les Brown. He always says, "When life knocks you on the ground, try to land on your back. If you can look up, you can get up. Let your reason get you back up."

Life Lesson

Notice, he did not say, "If" life knocks you on the ground. He said, "When," because it will. The difference between who survives and who doesn't is your will and reason to get back up. Getting up is not easy, but it is necessary. You must be intentional about it. The reality is that you have been given an assignment in this life. You must be deliberate about getting it done. Do not entertain negative feelings that may arise. Just do it! Keep moving forward and giving it your best effort, as my friend from years ago told me.

Knowing that you have a purpose is freeing. It allows you to stand tall among your peers. It makes a once-unconfident person very confident. When you understand your value as a person, you don't cower down. You are keenly aware that you bring something to the table. Don't get me wrong. Having a purpose does not make you arrogant or cause you to become insensitive to the feelings, thoughts, and opinions of others. On the contrary, it causes respect for humanity. You understand that all lives have meaning.

No one is better than the next person. However, as individuals, we must not water down our reason for being on this earth. Yes, we must support each other and assist wherever we can. Simultaneously, understand we have a job to do. We are on a journey, and a prize awaits at the end—eternal life. Therefore, we must be strategic as we live this life daily. We must assess the pros and cons of the choices we make. We must keep our eyes on the prize.

Many things will come to distract us. Sometimes, we go through things that make us feel like we can't go on. However, we must not yield to that feeling. It is just a feeling, and it is a lie. We can go on as long as we have God on our side and breath in our bodies.

I am reminded of the poem "Footprints in the Sand." At first, there are two sets of footprints in the sand where the person walked with God. Then, suddenly, one set of footprints remains. Those footprints belong to God. He is carrying His child, but both still move forward. I don't believe that the person God is carrying has given up. I think God knew they needed to feel Him as the friend that sticks closer than a brother.

God is always there. He will never leave or forsake you. He will be there when all the others turn their backs and leave you. This is one of the reasons I love Him so much.

He makes sure that I know He is right there with me when others are not. He motivates and encourages me, and He will do the same for you.

> A man that hath friends must show himself friendly: and there is a friend that sticketh closer than a brother.
>
> *Proverbs 18:24*

I know what it feels like not to be celebrated for who you are. Therefore, I am quick to celebrate others. A sign of maturity is when we can support and cheer for others even when the support is not reciprocated. I am determined not to be duped by jealousy and comparison. If you are reading this right now and need someone in your corner to encourage you to fulfill your dreams, I am your girl. Regardless of who is with or against you, remember that you and God are the majority.

Are You Convinced?

We hear so many positive messages in this day and age. I am not knocking them. I think they are all great. My question would be, do we really believe in the power of these positive messages?

For years, I was told there was a plan for my life. There is a purpose for my life. I could do anything. As a child, my aunt told me these things, guiding me to purpose. For the life of me, I just could not see what she saw. I made myself so small because of all I had been through. As I look back, I guess I believed it in my head. I did not want to believe that my aunt would lie to me. Yet, I did not believe it in my core. I was not truly convinced. Thus, I know now that this is a "walk of faith."

Even though I could see purpose so clearly in others, I was blind when it came to my own manifestation of purpose. I could cheer for others, but I thought it was sinful to cheer for myself. Oh! How wrong I was. It was not until I began to read the Bible for myself that I started seeing God's value for me. Since He thought I was worth sending His son to die on the cross for me, surely it is okay for me to appreciate myself.

> For God so loved the world, that he gave his only Son, that whosoever believeth in him should not perish, but have everlasting life.
>
> *John 3:16*

Examine what you truly believe about yourself and the purpose for your life. Then measure it against the Word of God. I hope you find peace and confidence at some point in this process. See and appreciate the beautiful bows, ribbons, and tapestries of others. Do not neglect the beauty and giftings God has given you.

Remember, you're on the flight of your life. Yes! I said the flight of your life. You see, before the plane takes off, the stewardess offers this advice. During extreme turbulence, masks will fall from the overhead compartment. Place your mask on first before assisting someone else. Thus, it's not wrong to love yourself first.

It's important to catch your breath when needed. You were not made to do everything. You are responsible for accomplishing your God-given assignment. Seeing others around you do ten things while you do one or two can be very intimidating. That is okay; don't be moved. As long as you're doing what God requires of you, it's okay. We are built differently. Some people are built for ten things, while others are built for one thing. When we align our focus on God, we end up in the same place.

CHAPTER 2

Your Family Isn't Perfect

God Chose Them

Most of the kids in our family had nicknames, and for some ungodly reason, they branded me "Mess." Mind you, it has been my life-long work to debunk that awful pronouncement. I often wondered what circumstances equated to such an awful nickname. Back then, no one considered the power of words. If so, they may have called me Harmony or Sweetie—anything but "MESS."

Well, just like I cannot choose my nickname, we cannot choose our family. At best, we can only try not to live up to the negative expectations. I guess I am trying to say that we all have things about our lives we wish we could change. For example, we all have family members who have exemplified less than "stellar" behavior. Hidden within most families are alcoholics, drug dealers, manipulators, liars, cheaters, and so on. We cannot change who they are or the fact that we are related. We can only give them the gifts we were given—lots of love and prayer—and let God do the rest.

I used to look at other families and think they had it all together. Because of this perspective, I began to loathe my own family. I knew deep down that this was not proper thinking, but that is how I felt.

I have since gotten the revelation that God chose my lineage even as He chose the members of Jesus' family. I never read where Jesus was embarrassed about His lineage. Instead, He loved them right where they were. Sometimes, that can seem difficult when high levels of pain and trauma have damaged what otherwise would have been a beautiful relationship. I am continually learning that traumas from the past do not define you. You hold the pen and can write a different narrative for your future. The best result will come when the script aligns with the Father's will.

Life Lesson

The lie of the enemy is for you to believe that your family has to be perfect. Oh, how wrong to think that. God made everyone. Therefore, treat them as God's treasure. We should not write off negative family members. However, there should be healthy boundaries because at the end of the day, your sanity takes priority.

As I was saying, God does not disown us for our imperfections. If so, we would be most miserable. I love how He takes time for everyone, regardless of status or stature. His love is unconditional and very tangible.

Sometimes, we treat others better than we treat our own family. Parents will downplay the gifts and talents of their own children while building up others. Wives will point out the strengths of someone else's husband and disregard their own. Husbands will open car doors, show respect to other women, and disrespect their own mothers, wives, and daughters. That is just ridiculous. It is like taking gas out of your own car and putting it in someone else's tank.

> I will praise thee; for I am fearfully and wonderfully made: Marvelous are thy works; And that my soul knoweth right well.
>
> *Psalm 139:14*

The Word tells us we are fearfully and wonderfully made. That word isn't just for everybody else. It pertains to you and everything that is attached to you. God chose your family specifically, and that makes them special.

Treat your family with the dignity and respect they deserve. There is a reason God made them a part of your life. Don't lose sight of that. If you do, you will regret it later. Sometimes, family is all you have when times are tough. Let them know you appreciate them. Hug them if you can, and tell them you love them. You may not be able to have that kind of relationship with some of them. That's okay. Do your part and move on. Keep your peace. God chose them to be connected to you.

No Shame

Due to the impact of living in an environment of poverty, I took on a negative persona. I thought every family was better than our family. We didn't have all the material bells and whistles that, in my eyes, made for a nice life. I felt so ashamed, mostly because I was poor with a "family drama" complex. At the time, I did not realize that no perfect family existed.

Trust was a big deal for me. If you lost my trust and respect, it was hard to get it back. I hated to be lied to or disappointed. I could pretty much tell if the people in my life were lying or telling the truth because I studied people. That is why, to this very day, I keep my word, especially to children. I am very intentional about that. A child will never forget that you made a promise and didn't keep it.

Anyway, I was a pretty friendly child and solidified a place for myself as an "old soul" or the "black sheep" in the family. The terms may vary depending on who you talk to. I had a few fights with my cousins here and there, but there was no denying that I had wisdom beyond my years. I loved hanging around the older folk. They were always talking, and I was always listening—listening and learning about what to do and what not to do. Don't get me wrong. I made my share of mistakes. However, I firmly believe that I made a lot less because I sat at the feet of those who had been there, done that, and got several t-shirts to show for it.

We were poor—my mom, dad, brother, and me—mainly because my dad had an alcohol addiction, not because he didn't work hard. The problem occurred when he got paid. He spent it all on alcohol. I never knew what drove him to drink. Was it because he grew up without a father? Was it because his family was poor? Was it a lack of love in this cold, hard world? All of these are possibilities and may have caused that outcome. At any rate, we often came home to a house with no electricity or water. In those days, when they turned the power off, my dad knew how to turn it right back on.

Then, there would be times when we would come home, and all our belongings would be sitting in the street. Life was hard back then. I remember the four of us walking the streets at night, trying to find someone to take us in. Oh, how I hated that feeling. It was just shameful. Sometimes one of our grandparents would let us in, but not before giving my parents a good tongue-lashing about the state of our lives. If the truth be told, some days I wanted to give them one, too. Yes, those days were rough, but I feel that they inspired me to strive for more in my life.

Life Lesson

Don't let the circumstances of your life drive you to do things that will cause harm to you or your family. Addictions are serious, and once you are addicted to anything, it can control and destroy your life if you don't put a stop to it.

My dad was strong, and instead of being made to feel ashamed, he needed love and support. Be a source of comfort and strength for the men God has placed in your life. Don't judge them or put them down. This world has already done that.

> There is therefore now no condemnation to them which are in Christ Jesus, who walk not after the flesh, but after the Spirit.
>
> *Romans 8:1*

God doesn't want us to walk with our heads hung down in guilt and shame. He did not send Jesus to shame us. He came to liberate us.

I am not saying that my dad was perfect and should not have been held accountable. However, I want to emphasize that there are many ways to inspire greatness in someone without shaming or crushing their spirit.

Flowers While They Live

Going to school was the worst. I don't think I brushed my teeth for the first few years (when I did get teeth). I remember many times using a wet rag and my finger. It is truly by God's grace that I have fairly good teeth today. We couldn't afford anything. I remember being so embarrassed when the teachers would look at me with eyes of pity. My hair wasn't combed. There were many days when I was dirty, with sleep in my eyes and grime under my fingernails. Not to mention the way I must have scarfed down the free breakfast and lunch meals. To this day, I miss Carnation breakfast bars and peanut butter sandwiches with honey.

In elementary school, reading was a struggle for me. Mind you, neither of my parents finished high school. My mother was forced to quit school in the 6th grade to assist my great-grandmother with the chores. I can only assume that my dad quit because he got into the wrong crowd and began drinking and partying.

Life Lesson

Never sacrifice your child's future to help someone else. The child might believe their life does not matter as much as the person you are trying to please. My mother missed out on a good education because she was forced to obtain adult responsibilities too soon. My father's lifestyle choices cost him his family. In my opinion, that was a gift that was too precious to lose. Good friends are great, but the wrong kind of friends will lead you down a dark path of ruin and destruction.

Anyway, I struggled with reading, and there was no help for me at home. The primary focus was survival, food, and a place to sleep at night. Thankfully, I had a concerned teacher named Ms. Mitchell. She noticed I had trouble reading and put me in a reading lab. I thank God for teachers who pay attention to their students.

I recall distinctly being in a circle on the floor. We were taking turns reading. For months, I could not connect the dots that would improve my reading. Then one day, I got it! My entire world lit up. I was reading. I felt like I could do anything. All because someone took the time to help me. My teacher did not see me as a "mess." She saw me as Precedere, a trailblazer, and someone with great potential. Now, here I am, an author, and you're reading my book.

Parents, if you are reading this, take time to help your children. If you can't, please enlist someone who can. It is very important that you don't give up on them. Eventually, things will click for them as they did for me. We have to look at the big picture when it comes to our children. The Bible teaches us to train up a child in the way he should go, and when he is old, he will not depart from it. The key objective is training. Training takes time. It takes effort. It takes attention. If we don't do these things, we can't expect to see the desired result. I know you work, go to school, etcetera. However, we owe our children an opportunity for a good start in life. Can you tell this is my soapbox? Ok, I digress.

Life has taught me that if my parents knew better, they would have done better as it relates to my upbringing. So, I have forgiven them and made the best of my situation. Forgiveness and letting things go are the best medicines. Truly, all things have worked out for my good, and I am better for it. In the words of Andy Stanley, "It has taught me to make better decisions with my own family so that I have fewer regrets today."

I am convinced that it takes a village to raise a family. I can remember looking up to my uncles as a strong cover for the family. My grandmothers (paternal and maternal) were once married, separated, and then divorced. I never knew my grandfathers. So, the sons they left behind had to become the protectors of the family.

An example of their assumed role would be when my mom and dad had a fight. My uncles would go look for my dad to beat him up. I remember being so bothered with my mom sometimes because I thought she was the reason they were attacking my dad. I don't know if that was the total truth, but it was my perspective at the time. FYI, that is all water under the bridge, now and I LOVE MY MOM!

Life Lesson

If you have an issue with your spouse, don't drag your family members in to resolve it. It only makes matters worse. In addition, it may breed contention and cause your kids to resent you and your family.

But yes, because there were no male role models, my uncles were forced into a role they were not prepared for. They smoked, drank, cursed, and womanized. Yet, family was everything to them, and they would put it all on the line for us.

Now, my aunts were there for us, too. My mom's sisters began to follow Christ when I was very young. One of her sisters was a preacher. Her name was Donette. Early on, she was an example for me. Aunt Donette was married with four kids. She and her husband opened up their home for Bible study and choir rehearsal every week.

I remember going to her house every Monday night. They would sing and pray. This was one of the first places I began to get to know the Lord. This is a precious memory to me to this very day. I am so thankful for their obedience and their willingness to take the time to share the Word with us. This particular aunt was such a symbol of strength in my life. She was bold and courageous, and she declared the Word with power and authority. She didn't seem fearful of anything, and it intrigued me. I really admired Aunt Donette. She gave me one of my first examples of an entire family living under the same roof and loving the Lord. It did my heart good; I was able to thank her before she went on to glory.

My youngest maternal aunt gave me a great awakening. Her name is Juanita. She told me if I died without knowing Jesus, I would go to hell. After she enlightened me at the tender age of 7 or 8, I really tried to walk the straight and narrow road. I don't know if it was her intent to scare the hell out of me, but she sure did.

Aunt Juanita was somewhat of the family's historian. She would tell me all the stories about the past. I just loved to sit and hear her talk about all the family history. She genuinely loved me and would give me inspiration to do better. She told me God had a plan for my life. Her words kept me from going down the wrong path.. Her wisdom has followed me to this day. By spending time with her I became distinctly aware of my decisions, and I possessed a strong awareness of right and wrong.

All my maternal aunts and uncles have since passed on. And I keep their memories. Even still, there are times I can't believe they are all gone. Going home to North Carolina is not the same without visiting them. However, they left me with great memories and a glowing hope in Christ. I know one day we will be together again.

I have one aunt remaining. (My dad's baby sister) I am her namesake. Yes, her name is Precedere. My mother loved her name so much that she decided to give it to me, and I am forever grateful. We used to have great conversations while she was pressing my hair. I remember her being somewhat of an entrepreneur as well. She would sell hard cups, clean people's houses, cook, and she was an avid reader. I still treasure the lessons I learned from her, til this day.

Life Lesson

Value the time you have with your family. Listen intently, love deeply, and carry the wisdom you have learned from them in your heart and use it.

My dad passed away also, but I have no regrets. Whenever I talked to him, I'd try to make him feel special. No blame.

No shame. I gave him his flowers while he lived. We have to do that, you know. I remember ignorantly thinking I would never be without him or any of my loved ones, for that matter. However, here I am writing this book, and some of them are gone. Love now, while you can. Display acts of kindness now. Let them smell the flowers of your care and concern for them. No, family is perfect, but we all deserve to be loved. Regret is a horrible thing. Saying I should have, I would have, or I could have does not leave a sense of peace in your heart. However, knowing you did your best to treat them with love, dignity, and respect goes a long way. So, give them flowers while they live.

CHAPTER 3

Be Yourself

"To thine ownself be true."

I have heard this statement several times over the course of my life. It is a statement from a scene in the award-winning stage play "Hamlet." In the scene, Polonius is bidding his son farewell. In doing so, he gives him this advice. In essence, Polonius was telling his son that success in life is found in being true to himself. By default, if he were to be true to himself, he would be true to others as well.

I can't help but wonder why he found it necessary to deposit such a statement in his son's psyche. He must have known that somewhere down the road, his son would encounter temptations that would cause him to question who he was. In instances where his core beliefs are challenged, he has to decide what is right and what is wrong for himself. In those times, the son would need to know it was okay to simply be honest and true to himself.

Haven't we all been there? If not, just keep living. I can only hope that when those times arise, we will stick to the moral fabric of who God created us to be. I pray we will not be influenced by the lies and deception this world has to offer. It is so easy to lose who we are in the world around us.

Whether it is our jobs, family, social media, educational pursuits, and so much more, we must realize God created us to be self-aware. He did not create us to be self-absorbed. However, we are not to discount who He has made us to be. Our thoughts matter. Our opinions matter. In short, we matter. If to no one else, we matter to God.

Learn to enjoy the sound of your own voice. It has taken me some time to love and appreciate my own voice because I would downplay my own thoughts to be in agreement with someone else's. The day I stopped downplaying my thoughts, I began to walk in so much freedom.

Being likable to everyone is overrated and exhausting. I came to the realization that I am not in a circus, and I don't have to do tricks to please anyone. Besides, God did not create me for that purpose. Now, I want you to know that, just as Polonius told his son, you will walk in your true purpose when you have learned to face the truths and realities of who you are.

If you accept yourself, others will follow suit. This is the biggest obstacle. Our default seems to focus on all our flaws. Yet none of them have caught our God by surprise. So, embrace them—every stinking one of them.

Life Lesson

God created you. Therefore, He knew your flaws were there. They are a part of the fabric of who you were, who you are now, and who you will eventually become. Don't try to explain them away or make excuses for their existence. We are all flawed, born in sin, and shaped in iniquity.

My friend, this is not the sum total of you. It is only a part of you.

Now, let's talk about the beauty that lies within you. Yes, let's speak of the good qualities you possess. You are beautiful. You have the ability to create and turn negatives into positives. You are full of light and love. You are funny and witty and have the capacity to create wonderful, long-lasting relationships. You are not arrogant, but confident. After all, why shouldn't you be? The God of the universe created you smart, talented, and funny. Yes, all of these wonderful traits and more belong to you.

I want you to see that the good in you outweighs the bad. So be you. Don't lie to yourself. Don't try to be someone else. Doing so is an insult to the God Who created you. He makes no mistakes. The best way to show that you appreciate His creation is by being the absolute best you that you can be.

Reflection in the Mirror

So God created man in his own image, in the image of God created He him, male and female created he them.

Genesis 1:27

Who are you? Who do you see when you look in the mirror? This may seem like an odd question to ask, but I submit to you that it is a very important question. In order to have a successful life, there are a few things we must come to grips with about ourselves.

First of all, we are children of God, and we were created

in His image. We were created in His "spiritual" likeness. Therefore, we are to be like Him. An image is a reflection. We often hear the term WWJD (What Would Jesus Do?). Our lives should mirror the Son of God because the Son mirrors the Father.

I love the phrase WWJD because it is a gauge for us. Jesus is the ultimate example of how we should live our lives. Jesus is just like God, and His biggest desire was to please His heavenly Father. That should be our desire as well. The Bible tells us to honor the Lord with all of our hearts and lean not to our own understanding. We are to acknowledge God in all of our ways, and He will direct our path.

When we ask, "What would Jesus do?", we are acknowledging our Father in a deep personal way. We are asking Him to guide us on His path for our lives. There is no one more qualified to lead us than God. He knows the way, and He will bring us home safely.

Have you ever looked at your reflection in the water? Did the person looking back at you seem familiar? I have had the experience of staring at myself and feeling like I did not even know the person looking back at me. Now, that is a weird feeling. If we can feel that way as humans looking at our own reflection, can you imagine how God must feel when He looks at us and we don't resemble Him at all?

Every parent wants to see themselves in their child, especially fathers. If there is no resemblance, questions about relationships can arise. Even as a mother, when my adult children are around, I find myself staring at them, looking for similarities confirming what I already know—

they are mine. My heart knows they are a part of me, and I get filled with so much joy. This is what God must have felt when He asked Satan if he had considered His servant Job. Why did God brag about Job? Could it be that Job was a reflection of Him on earth? I believe God had a "proud Papa moment." May God be our mirror and show us who we are.

Meet the Press

And be not conformed to this world, but be ye transformed by the renewing of your mind that ye may prove what is that good and acceptable and perfect will of God.

Romans 12:2

In most cases, when we humans make our entrance into the world, there is a grand announcement. Likewise, God shared the news of Jesus' birth in Matthew 2:1-2. "Now when Jesus was born in Bethlehem of Judea in the days of Herod the king, behold there came wise men from the east to Jerusalem. Saying, 'Where is he that is born King of the Jews? For we have seen his star in the east and have come to worship him.'"

It spread abroad that Jesus would be arriving, and the press (people) had already assembled. In our day, the paparazzi would have been on the scene. The cameras would have been rolling. There would have been photo ops, news blogs, Facebook posts, and Instagram posts. You name it; every form of social media would have been engaged. One could consider this a good thing, but don't get it twisted; there would be sinister workings in the background. All press is not good press. King Herod was watching the news. Also, he wanted to kill the King of kings and the Lord of lords.

I'm using this analogy to let you know we have our own press. Some of us were given lavish baby showers and gatherings to prepare for our arrival. Early on, we would have been greeted with lavish gifts and more hugs and kisses than we could wrap our heads around. The Press Corp. would include Grandma's, Papa's, Aunts, Uncles, Cousins, Godparents, and a host of friends and family.

Nevertheless, as we grow up, the exuberance of being born fades. Eventually, life goes on. Then, you learn that human love is centered on circumstances and conditions. Yet, God's love remains with you forever. Don't get me wrong. Your family and friends will be there, but the newness of "you" will wear off. They will love you, but will they be enthralled by you? Not so much. Oh, boy, let us not forget about your enemies. The chief of them is the devil himself. He hated Jesus. So please understand that you are no different.

Life Lesson

The lesson I am trying to convey is that there is a reason to celebrate your birth, just as there was for Jesus. He was born with a purpose, and that was to save us from our sins. Albeit, He was not welcomed by all, and we won't be either. He was celebrated. He was hated. However, He was not deterred from His assignment.

You were uniquely crafted by God, and you were born with a purpose. Stay focused on that purpose. You have your own "positive" press corps. Those who will support the reason you were born will give you the Atta-boys and proverbial pats on the back. When that happens, embrace it. It is necessary and will help you get through the times when your "negative" press corps is on duty. What did you say? You mean, I will get some negative press? "Yes, ma'am" and "Yes, sir." You will not be loved by everyone. Jesus was loved deeply, but He was also hated greatly. It is to our advantage to make peace with this inevitable truth about life.

One more thing: "Squash the press." Essentially, what I am saying is to be indifferent to it. Whether it is good or bad, do not engage in the "ups and downs" of people's opinions of who you are. People's perceptions of you will change like the wind. They will love you with one breath and hate you with the next. Even Peter told Jesus he would never deny Him, but would later say, "I never knew the man." The beauty of this is that Jesus was indifferent to the change in Peter's perception of who He was and loved him anyway.

That seems to be asking a lot—to love, even when you are being persecuted. I am not saying it's easy. Lord knows, it is not. We cannot do this on our own. We need God's help. When we notice the disturbing indicators of negative press in our lives, we must pray. Pray not just for ourselves, but for the people who are pushing the negativity. Really, they are the ones who need our prayers the most.

I have heard this multiple times, and it is true: "Hurt people, hurt people." People who have open wounds in their own lives often lash out at other people. They have not experienced the God who gives peace that surpasses understanding. Nevertheless, the Lord said He would be with you. He will not leave or forsake you. He will be there for others as well, but they have to be open to receiving Him. He also said if we would acknowledge Him in all our ways, He would direct our path. So, acknowledge the Father. Allow Him to show you how to manage the media in your life and give you peace.

I have noticed over the course of my life that good deeds are seldom noticed. No one shouts your good deeds from the rooftop. Well, usually they won't. Don't let that move you. Visualize God standing in the bleachers of your life, applauding your efforts and deeds of righteousness.

This is the real truth. You are what God says about you. Do not entertain anything that opposes this single truth. Romans 12:2 tells us to renew our minds. We are not to conform to the world's perception of us. We are to keep our minds fresh and up-to-date with the information God has given us about who we are. Then, we may succeed in fulfilling His purpose and destiny for our lives.

Do life as you. No one can beat you at being you. You have the advantage. Be who God created you to be. Be yourself, and your reward will be great.

CHAPTER 4

People on Your Path

Those who Teach

Life is a journey. The beauty of life is that we don't have to do it alone. God has put people on this earth who are doing just what we are doing. While "traveling through," we will never meet everyone who is taking the journey with us. Yet, God has put those we encounter on our path specifically for us. We will laugh with some and cry with others. We will attend weddings, baby showers, funerals, and even work with some travelers. These interactions are not to be taken lightly. They are to be embraced to receive the seed found in every relationship. Either they will deposit something into our lives or we will make a deposit into theirs.

I have met many people throughout the course of my life. Over time, I have become very intentional, so I can be sensitive to what I should learn from my interactions with them and what I can teach. Yes, you read it correctly. We are teachers because someone is learning from your life—what to do or what not to do. I know that reality comes with a little pressure, but it is true. In fact, part of our purpose is to "teach" the right lessons.

Teach is defined as "to show or explain how to do something." Some synonyms for teach are discipline, educate, instruct, school, and train. We are always learning, so that means something is always being taught. Let's take a pause here to think about the teachers God has allowed into our path, whether good or bad.

I learned to respect older people from my mother. I passed that nugget of wisdom down to my own children as well. There is much to be said about the people who were here before us. Their experiences can help us avoid making their mistakes. The tragedy of this generation is their reluctance to listen to the elders. Be advised; the lessons are coming. They will either come from a person (someone who cares enough to point you in the right direction) or they will come through life experiences (the school of hard knocks).

While my husband and I were stationed at Fort Knox in Kentucky, we decided that I would stay at home with our toddler daughter until she went to school. Well, as time went on, I wanted to altar that plan. Because all my friends worked outside the home, I felt it necessary to do the same. Now, there was nothing wrong with my desire. However, it was not God's plan for me at the time.

Well, my neighbor was a manager at the gas station. So, I decided I would submit an application to get a job where she worked. As you might have guessed, I got the job. My husband didn't agree with my getting a job, but I thought he didn't want me to have a career (I know better now).

I told him that he was standing in the way of my destiny. I said, "The door of opportunity is open for me, and I am going to walk right through it." Well, needless to say, I should have listened to him. The experience was not great. Only a gas station attendant would understand the crazy hours and diverse characters that frequent this type of business. To this day, I have great respect for the people who work there. My point is that God puts people on our path to point us in the right direction. These people care about us, and if we listen, we will not have to experience those "hard knocks."

Mortal Mentors

Titus 2 has to be one of my favorite chapters in the Bible.

1 But speak thou the things which become sound doctrine:
2 That the aged men be sober, grave, temperate, sound in faith, in charity, in patience.
3 The aged women likewise, that they be in behaviour as becometh holiness, not false accusers, not given to much wine, teachers of good things;
4 That they may teach the young women to be sober, to love their husbands, to love their children,
5 To be discreet, chaste, keepers at home, good, obedient to their own husbands, that the word of God be not blasphemed.
6 Young men likewise exhort to be sober minded.
7 In all things shewing thyself a pattern of good works: in doctrine shewing uncorruptness, gravity, sincerity,

8 Sound speech, that cannot be condemned; that he that is of the contrary part may be ashamed, having no evil thing to say of you.

9 Exhort servants to be obedient unto their own masters, and to please them well in all things; not answering again;

10 Not purloining, but shewing all good fidelity; that they may adorn the doctrine of God our Saviour in all things.

11 For the grace of God that bringeth salvation hath appeared to all men,

12 Teaching us that, denying ungodliness and worldly lusts, we should

live soberly, righteously, and godly, in this present world;

13 Looking for that blessed hope, and the glorious appearing of the great God and our Saviour Jesus Christ;

14 Who gave himself for us, that he might redeem us from all iniquity, and purify unto himself a peculiar people, zealous of good works.

15 These things speak, and exhort, and rebuke with all authority. Let no man despise thee.

I find myself quoting this chapter a lot in my conversations. I love the principles it represents. This chapter displays mentorship in its finest form. I firmly believe everyone needs to find themselves some good role models—people who are actually living and displaying a righteous life.

As I stated earlier, God will put people in your path to show you the right way. Learn to recognize them in your life and glean from their wisdom. I told you that my mother used to tell us to listen to older people. It was her way of pointing us in the right direction. My mother was not present in my life for many years. However, her sound instruction remained with me. She is absolutely right. I have learned so many things by just taking the time to listen to "Mortal Mentors." Even still, there have been many times I have learned things the hard way.

> Train up a child in the way he should go, and he will not stray when he is old.
>
> *Proverbs 22:6*

Again, "teach" means to show the way, discipline, educate, instruct, school, and train. It is so important to train your children to listen to wise counsel. If left to their own devices, most likely, they will fail miserably in life. Proverbs 29:15 solidifies this statement. It says, "The rod and reproof give wisdom; but a child left to himself bringeth his mother to shame."

As parents, my husband and I had the same goals as it relates to rearing our children. We taught them the principles of the Word of God. There are a lot of tools available for raising children, and to be honest, we have used a few of them. However, our primary source is the Bible. It has been proven over thousands of years, and in short, it works.

We are to train our children. Now, in the process of training them, we will definitely learn something. I have learned so many things about and from my children. The most important lesson for me has been that although I gave birth to them, they are not mine. They belong to God, just as Jesus did not belong to Mary. She was a steward and a caretaker. She fed Him, clothed Him and gave Him shelter until He was able to go out on His own.

It bothers me to see parents who fail to check their children's bad behavior. Why, you may ask. Well, for one thing, it teaches the kids there are no consequences (that's not true). Also, the child could receive a false sense of entitlement. Even if you give your child a pass for misbehaving, the world will not be so kind.

Even Mary checked Jesus when He fell away from the group to go teach in the temple. Although He was doing good work, He humbled Himself and became submissive to His mother.

The book of Titus admonishes the older men to teach the younger men, and likewise, the older women to teach the younger women. This is a piece of advice that seems to be missing in our society today. People are immersed in self-preservation, not even considering the next generation.

We tend to think we will live forever, but the truth of the matter is that we will not. We will live on through the legacy we leave behind. So let us do as Paul commissioned us in the book of Titus. We must share the lessons we have learned in order to help the next generation succeed in life. The Bible tells us if we know to do good and we don't do it, then we are in sin. Don't be selfish; do the good that you can while you are here.

Teaching others is sometimes easier said than done because we are in a battle to be heard. Sometimes, we literally talk until we are blue in the face. It is not because we love to hear ourselves talk. It is because the love that we have and God's love for this next generation run deep.

There is a plea on the inside of us that wants what is best. There is also a life-load of lessons within us that we want to share. We cringe when we see younger folks about to make the same errors we did. It is so unnecessary. I beg the younger folks, please listen. Doing so will spare you a lot of drama and headaches. A little patience is all that is required. Just hear us out and then make your decision. However, just by listening, you showed respect and reverence for the older person, who, in their own way, was trying to give you some good advice.

Life Lesson

Take note of the people God places in your life. He created every single one of them with purpose, just as He did with you. Sometimes, their purpose is intermingled with yours. There is something for you to learn from them, or vice versa. However, if we walk around treating every encounter as just a frivolous interaction, we will miss the blessing God has for us.

Sometimes, God may put a person in our lives to warn us of danger. On the other hand, He may have someone there to bless us, financially or in other ways. I remember moving to a different city. We enrolled my son in the school there. He ran track at his previous school and wanted to participate at the new school, as well. However, we had a problem. Due to my husband and my work schedule, our son didn't have transportation after track practice. Well, God put a person in our lives (Mother Vera Mays). She was glad to help. God knows what we need, when we need it, and who can give it to us. Remember, your footsteps are ordered by the Lord, and you must be mindful of the people He places in your path.

Chapter 5

Find Christ Find Life

When I was nine years old, my brother and I became wards of the state. This means our sole custody was taken from my parents. My father's addiction to alcohol and the fussing and fighting between him and my mom had taken their toll on our family. As a result, we moved into foster care.

My mother left the state to go live with people I did not know. I would not physically see her again until I graduated high school. Additionally, my dad made the choice to enter a rehab facility. After that, I don't recall ever seeing or hearing of him taking another drink.

In the meantime, hopelessness crept its way into my life. All my dreams of having a real family (whatever that entailed) seemed to disappear. All our belongings were packed up, and everyone went their separate ways. During that time, I vowed that if I ever had kids, I would never leave them.

It was a painful situation. It left a deep scar in my heart and in my life. I will forever thank my Lord and Savior, who is the mender of broken hearts. Over time, He has gently restored the shattered pieces of my life.

Moving forward, I began to cultivate feelings of rejection. I felt no one cared that I existed. As a ward of state, I was in the system. My relationships felt like some sort of business transaction. Now I know that was not true. Nevertheless, my perspective seemed real.

There are people who really care and are willing to make "foster" kids part of their own family. I have a healthy respect for these precious souls to this very day. I recall, in the deep recesses of my mind, hearing the voice of Jesus saying, "I love you." Amazingly, through all the noise, I could still hear my Lord's voice. He was gently conveying that He had a purpose and a planned destiny for my life. I can't explain it, but I knew He was watching over us while my parents were finding themselves.

I know my parents believed in God, and deep down, I knew they believed in prayer. Surely someone, somewhere, was praying for us. Looking back on things, it is funny how, while drinking, my parents sang gospel songs. It was as if they knew Jesus as their Lord and Savior. Sometimes, they would even sing in unison.

As a youngster, I judged them so harshly. Truthfully, I thought they were old enough to make better decisions. In actuality, they were really very young. Now, I cherish the moments we had, even though they were brief. I don't miss the drinking and fussing, but I do miss the togetherness.

My dad has since passed. I remember foolishly thinking my parents would live forever. I've learned that none of us do. I can't honestly say that I knew my dad's spiritual state when he died. However, I just know I love and miss him. As for his relationship with God, that was between him and God. Even still, I sure hope I get to see him in heaven. I hope he found eternal life in Christ.

In his later years, my dad would call me just about every day. Although, at times, it seemed a bit overwhelming to see that we had never built a real relationship. Anyway, I never dismissed the calls. In some weird way, it seemed those calls were apologies for the decisions he made when we were young. It was his way of saying, "I love you."

God gave me wisdom to never throw the past in his face. Instead, I showed him the same love and forgiveness shown to me by a loving God. What would it have accomplished, anyway? We cannot change the past, but we can change the future.

Life Lesson

Parents, your decisions impact your entire family. So, do your best to make wise ones. Other people can take care of your children, but nothing replaces a parent's love. When mending broken relationships, you may never receive a verbal apology (it may not be necessary). In the process, just appreciate every act of kindness shown.

Only God knows a person's heart. No one is perfect. Everyone will make their share of mistakes. Be quick to forgive and move on. Lastly, when you let Christ into the corridors of your heart, He does the work required to make you whole again. No matter what life has thrown your way, Jesus specializes in breathing life into dead situations.

We didn't stay in foster care for long. It was maybe a year or two, at the most. My dad's mom did the paperwork required to get us out of the system and back with the family.

By the time I went to stay with my grandmother, I figured I knew what life was all about. I decided I couldn't trust anyone. My philosophy was that if my parents could leave me, no one else could truly be trusted. I would soon come to realize that trust should be in God and not in man. Humans have good intentions. They mean well, but we are fallible. God is infallible. When you find Him, you will have an anchor that will never leave or fail you.

Anyway, I became somewhat of a rebel, still reeling from the pain of a broken home. I always wanted a traditional family—the entire family under the same roof. However, my dreams were shattered, and I kind of lost hope. Then I started looking for love in all the wrong places.

I tried a few ungodly vices, only resulting in more pain. Thank God, the vices didn't stay with me. I could never figure out the hype about drinking. I saw its destructive effects firsthand and wanted nothing to do with them. Again, this was another way God was looking out for me, and I didn't even realize it. I became angry at the very thought of drinking, smoking, etc. and vowed never to use them because they destroyed my family. Drugs may seem cool, but they are not.

I recall once that my mother kept us from school to join her friends and relatives in the park. All the adults were partying and drinking. Then someone got the bright idea to let the kids join in on the fun. My cousin and I may have been seven or eight years old. We were given beer and cigarettes. While in a drunken state, my cousin and I started burning each other with cigarettes. To this day, I have the burn marks over my eye to prove it...lol   Thank God that she didn't burn my eyeball. Many years later, she passed. I know she would get a real kick out of my writing about this story.   She and I used to reminisce and laugh about this alot.

Life Lesson

Don't involve your kids in activities that are unsafe or where they are too young to be involved. This includes conversations. There are some things that are not appropriate for kids. Allow God to show you how to raise them. Let them be children as long as they can. They will grow up soon enough, and they can't recapture their younger years.

Illuminated by the Spirit

Up to a certain point, I had only flirted with a relationship with God. I would soon learn that true prosperity is "peace of mind." The world I entered came with a lot of pain and heartache. The people I thought I could trust and who would love me forever were not the superheroes I envisioned. Instead, they were just earthly, flawed individuals. By golly, they were human.

Once God opened my eyes to my dependency on the wrong people, it relieved so much pressure from my life. I wanted someone to blame for all the things I thought were wrong in my life. When, in fact, the common denominator in every scenario of my life was me. The only person who can be blamed for what happens in my life now is me.

Life Lesson

Don't put anyone on a pedestal. We are all human beings with the potential to disappoint and make mistakes. Being dependent on others for the outcome of your life is a cowardly tool. It is used so you can blame others when things go wrong. Don't use blame as a crutch. Ask God to be your guide in life, and He will show you the path you should take. He will illuminate your path to your purpose.

Moving forward, my emotions were all over the place. I was too inexperienced to handle what was handling me. Life had become a series of highs and lows. My identity had been wrapped up in so many things. I didn't have a clear view of who I was. Finally, it dawned on me: I needed to find a friend, a guide, and a mentor. I needed to find Christ.

Back then, Christ caught so many of my tears and showed me so much mercy. I didn't even know Him like I do now, but He was right there all the time. He was working on my heart and bringing light to my dark situations.

You may ask, How did you know He was working on things? Well, I'm glad you asked. If I may be honest, most of the time, I was pleading for Him to show up on my behalf. I did not see Him working, but that does not mean He wasn't.

I wanted Him to work things out in a way that suited

me, but my ways are not His ways. Oh, how grateful I am for that. Cakes baked with love from scratch taste so much better than store-bought ones. God, through His Holy Spirit, is still using my life's ingredients and making a dessert pleasing to the palate. Although He is my Maker, I get to share in the process. As I listen and follow His instructions, we work hand in hand to create the best possible outcomes for my life. Oh, how I love Him. He is truly a friend who sticks closer than a brother.

Life Lesson

Find out who you are before trying to find value in someone else. If you love yourself first, then it won't matter if no one else does. If you're not being loved the way God would love you, please re-evaluate the connection and remove yourself from the relationship. You are too precious to be treated badly. Illumination happens when God gives you a prospect, idea, revelation, etc. that you did not have before. Let God open your eyes so you can see who you are in Him. Have a clear vision of His purpose and plan for your life.

Formed in the Fire

If there's one thing I've learned, life doesn't allow you to catch your breath. Life keeps on rolling along, and it will roll you right over if you let it. In a lot of ways, life is like being on a train that just keeps moving. It can also be likened to a fast-moving roller coaster ride. Everything in you wants to make it stop, but the wheels just keep on turning.

The advantage is having the power to tell yourself to

stop—wait a minute. You must be intentional about taking the time you need to think things through and make better choices. Life will not stop for you, but you can stop for yourself. So, you don't ruin your life by living carefree and foolishly.

I had a boyfriend whose parents were ministers. I now know that he was only in my life to help me truly come to Christ. I remember distinctly going to church with him, and the altar call was given. It seemed as if it was just me and God in that little church. I found myself in the middle of the aisle, just weeping. It was like the cause of my sorrow and shame were being stripped away.

The preacher spoke the sinner's prayer, and I repeated every word. For the first time, I understood my life needed to change. I needed to get serious about my relationship with God. I truly felt the Spirit of God loving me. At that point, I didn't need the approval of others. I was different. I was changed.

I found Christ, or, better put, He had found me. He was never lost. I was lost, hurt, broken, and rejected. He found me. Oh, how grateful I am! I finally had someone who would be with me forever. He would never leave me or forsake me. I could talk to Him about any and every issue that would present itself in my life. In short, I was saved. And, as it turned out, God had a separate path in mind for the young man who brought me to church.

Now that I was saved, I needed a mentor. I needed to be taught about this new life. Annie Knockett took me under her wing and showed me the ways of Christ. She picked me up and brought me to church. She showed me how to study the Bible, pray, and bring souls into God's kingdom. What a blessing she was in my life!

Annie was on fire for Christ, and I was her protege. I had never seen anyone love God the way she did. There was no room for compromise. She was not playing around. Annie's philosophy was either you were saved or not saved—going to heaven or hell. There was no in-between.

I was drawn to her passion for God, and I noticed a new-found love that caused me to weep in a satisfying and happy way. This love calmed my nerves. The material things in life didn't matter anymore. It was all about Him—Jesus Christ.

I had a part-time job at Hardee's fast-food establishment. I worked the drive through not long after getting saved. I looked out of the window, and the bushes just looked different. I looked at my hands; they looked different too. I knew I was different in a way that was and still is unexplainable. From that moment on, I wanted to help everyone find the life I found.

I was telling everyone about Jesus. Miss Knocket acted as my spiritual midwife. Again, she taught me how to pray and study the Word. She was the person who assisted me in receiving the Holy Ghost. She dressed me, fed me, and did my hair. I can never repay her for the kindness, but I know God will.

Annie owned a thrift store in the worst area of town. I worked with her for many days. Countless times, she took passersby to the back of the store and prayed with them to receive Jesus. It wasn't too long before I did the same—slaying demons and casting out devils. Annie was a firecracker, and I became one, too.

My family thought I had flipped my lid. They were the main ones I wanted to save. I just couldn't bear the thought of me being in heaven and them in hell. Well, they would have none of it. They branded me a holy roller and went about their merry way. However, that did not stop me from praying for them or spreading the Word to anyone who would listen. Being "saved" was a lonely existence at first, but eventually their hearts warmed up to me with God's help. Eventually, I gained their respect.

It is with love and kindness that God has drawn us to Himself. He desires us to draw others as well. Originally, I thought that in order to be a Christian, I had to disassociate myself completely from my old friends. Now, for a season, I needed separation. I wasn't better than anyone, but I needed to get a firm foundation before I could help anyone else. What I didn't realize was that the decision to separate for a season would have a consequence.

You see, I had a group of friends that were used to being around me. We had a whole group at school with T-shirts and everything. We had camaraderie. However, when I got saved, everything changed. I needed deliverance from so much; I didn't consider how the Christian lifestyle would impact my friends.

One thing is for sure: They respected my choice and did not try to change me. I knew they missed me. However, I understood it was best for them to see me go through this life-changing process.

Life Lesson

Sometimes in life, you will have to make decisions that are very uncomfortable. Most times, you will have to press forward alone. Nevertheless, those decisions take wisdom, especially when they affect your destiny. God loves everyone. We must be wise so we can win souls.

I guess what I am trying to say is that my life would be totally different had I not received Christ as my Lord and Savior. He has been my compass. He has been my guide. Things have not always been easy, but by His grace, goodness, and guidance, I am not a victim in this life. I am truly victorious. Hallelujah!

62

Chapter 6

Clap for Others

Our universal culture teaches us to give applause to the things that please us. Our appreciation could come in the form of a nod of the head, a smile, a hand clap, etc. We are trained to give a response that communicates that we are pleased with another's presentation.

This act of gratitude can and does mean so much to the person on the receiving end. While it feels good to get applause, it is equally disappointing when the performance is met with disdain, disgust, or displeasure. Now, I know we should not center our emotions around the appreciation of others for the gifts and talents we offer. However, if we are honest with ourselves, we would have to admit that it feels good to be appreciated.

There is nothing like adrenaline stimulated through "people pleasing." Please don't misunderstand my intent. I think it is wonderful to be "liked," but sometimes the term is overrated. There should be a balance concerning our care for others' reactions. If you care too little about the opinions of others, you can become arrogant and think you know everything, and my friend, it's simply not true. No one knows everything. We can learn from other people and hopefully not make the same mistakes they made.

On the other hand, if you care too much about the opinions of others, you begin to lose your own identity. There's a difference between healthy respect and high respect for other people. High respect moves you into imitating another person. You must remember that you will never be that person. By all means, clap for them and applaud their positive contributions, but don't devalue or downplay the amazing craftsmanship God used while creating you. So, learn to love and appreciate who you are while appreciating others as well.

There is an adrenaline rush when you are well received. There's the opposite effect when there are opposing views on your presentation. How do you feel when the preverbal egg is thrown, or you are booed off the stage? My friend, this is when you are really tested. Albeit, do not be devastated.

Honey Child (southern slang), you are something special. You're you-nique. If no one else applauds your efforts, go stand in front of the mirror. Give yourself the biggest smile. Take both of your hands, put them together, and begin to clap. Clap for your successes. Clap when you fail. Clap in disappointment. Clap for near misses. Clap because of every situation God has brought you through. Clap if He's currently bringing you through trials. I dare you to go ahead and clap.

It feels good to clap for yourself. So, do it often until it becomes a natural occurrence. Too often, we wait for other people to tell us we have done a good job. We sometimes crave for them to say it. Accolades from other people may never happen. So, give it to yourself. The Bible tells us to encourage ourselves because God has given us the power to do so.

It is important that we celebrate the achievements of others. Some people will love everything about you. They will think everything you do is great. Having these kinds of people in your life is wonderful. Everyone needs someone to be in their corner. However, you need to applaud yourself if no one else does.

Living for the applause of others defeats the beautiful purpose God has for your life. He created you in such a magnificent way. God wants you to stand even when no one else is standing with you. God is the only cheerleading squad you will ever need.

People will love you today and hate you tomorrow. It all depends on their mood. I have seen it happen so many times. They will laugh with you while it is convenient for them. Yet, they can change colors when someone they deem more important than you arrives on the scene. Beware of these types of people. They mean you no good.

True friends are people who will be with you for the long haul. They will not abandon you because of your financial status or the way you look, talk, or dress. Friends are loyal, and their love for you is real. I guess what I am trying to say is that a friend's love is deep, not shallow.

A friend will speak the truth, even if it means you may stop speaking to them. They are willing to risk the relationship in order to see you in a better place. In my opinion, a friend's love is similar to a mother's love. There is a story in the Bible that expresses this beautifully.

Outside of Jesus, King Solomon was the wisest man to ever live. The day came when he had to put his wisdom on display. Two women lived in the same house. Both women had newborn sons. One of the babies had been smothered, and both ladies appeared before Solomon, claiming ownership of the child that remained.

Solomon called for his sword so that the remaining child could be cut in two for each woman to receive half a child. The real mother screamed in anguish and said, "Don't kill the baby. Let her have him." Solomon saw the love of the woman in anguish and commanded the baby to remain in her care.

A friend's love (like a mother's love) can hurt, but a true friend makes sacrifices that will benefit you. This was a selfless act on the real mother's part. I am not saying anyone should make such a drastic sacrifice for you. However, real friends care enough to want the very best for you. This is how they "clap for you." This is how they applaud your life.

I've always been intentional about "clapping for others." I know how it feels when people who are close to you confess their love but are intentional about applauding everyone and not you. If you see this happening in your relationships, these people have taken you for granted. They think you will always be there for them. This kind of attitude shows they do not appreciate you.

I encourage you to look at your surroundings. Applaud the people who stick with you during the good and bad times. They are a gift given by God. So, don't use and abuse them, or you will lose them.

Life Lesson

People come and go. However, the good ones usually stay, and the bad ones eventually go. Deceitful people come with ulterior motives. Sadly, we are sometimes duped by them, becoming impressed by their presentation. We reserve a special place for them until something goes wrong. Eventually, they show us, as Maya Angelo said, "who they really are." After the smokescreen clears, we see who our true friends are. Sometimes it's the people we take for granted. Take the time to get to know the pillars in your life. These are the people who stick around. They are the true heroes. So, let's give them a hand.

As I write this, I am reminded of Saul and David. David was a good friend and would have given his life for Saul. However, Saul was blinded by rage and his unnecessary jealousy of David. Instead of applauding David's loyalty and friendship, Saul threw a javelin at him. Saul wanted to kill David! I can't help but wonder what their relationship would have been like if Saul recognized the treasure in David's friendship.

Life Lesson

Clapping for others does not diminish you. You are still the great, brilliant person God created. Remember that as you show genuine love and support for other people's gifts and talents, you will never know how one simple act of kindness can affect someone else's life. Some people don't have a cheering section. So, give someone a high-five, a pat on the back, a smile, or a nod of approval.

Maya Angelou stated, "When people show you who they are, believe them the first time." That's good advice. Make a mental note of when people are negative toward you. See it is a redirection, not a rejection. And don't let it rub off on you.

Apply the Golden Rule: treat others as you want to be treated. Continue to applaud even as David continued to play the harp for Saul. David eventually became the King of Israel. God's purpose for your life is being fulfilled, especially when you treat your enemies right.

Love your enemies, bless them that curse you, do good to them that hate you, and pray for them that despitefully use you, and persecute you. Matthew 5:44

Be the bigger person; clap for others. You may never know who needs a smile, a hug, or a kind word from you. Let the Lord use you to add sunshine to someone's gloomy day.

CHAPTER 7

Let There Be Space

As I contemplated this chapter, the word "space" leaped to the forefront of my mind. Miriam-Webster defines it "as a continuous area or expanse which is free, available, or unoccupied."

It is very important to have space or make room in your life for essential things. You can look at this from a few perspectives. One, space allows room in your life for things that bring you joy and cause you to grow. Sometimes we are so busy that we don't have time for anyone or anything. In this case, we need to create a space for things that are important.

I find myself scrambling for time a lot. Most of the time, it's due to a lack of planning, but that is another story. Today, let's talk about a few things that require room in our lives. First and foremost, we need to make time for God. We need to set aside time every day to honor the One who created us, the One who wakes us up every morning. Without Him, there would be no you or me.

Then, we should allow space for self-care. This includes,

but is not limited to, making room for exercise and eating right. Make time to do the things you love, whether it is sewing, reading, decorating, cooking, golfing, or watching a basketball game. A lot of the time, our default behavior is to put ourselves last. While that is necessary in some cases, it is not true all the time. We are valuable, and we need maintenance.

Finally, it is important to make time for others. Sometimes the hardships we face in life can cause us to feel like we don't need anyone. Let me inform you that that couldn't be farther from the truth. We need each other, so invite someone to lunch. Have a meaningful conversation with a friend. Make time to listen to others. These interactions can add so much value to your life.

On the flip side, too much fellowship can ruin relationships, and too much time spent alone will result in isolation. We must have healthy boundaries and balance in every aspect of our lives. This applies spiritually, emotionally, and physically.

Time for God

I cannot begin to tell you how many books I have purchased and read concerning spending time with God. There is so much information on this topic, and rightfully so. As a new-born Christian, I was told I had to spend time with God. The only problem was that I wasn't quite sure how to accomplish that goal. Although I knew spending time with Him was right, my efforts seemed fruitless.

Throughout the course of my life, I have been around people who have made spending time with God seem easy.

For instance, they would say things like, "I spent five hours in prayer or I fasted 30 days." Don't get me wrong. I am not knocking their connection with God. I think it is wonderful but intimidating at the same time. As a new Christian, I thought I had to do the same thing, or at least try to keep up. Now, I know better. Then I didn't.

There are so many ways to spend time with God. You can schedule time with God on your calendar and make it one of your regular appointments. You can start your day with God for a few minutes early in the morning. I'll admit, I tried early morning meetings with God as a young mother and failed miserably. I only accomplished beating the snooze button on my alarm clock to a pulp.

You can try using a Bible app on your phone. You can read through the Bible in a year. My husband does this every year. God bless him. He sets such a good example. You can join a small Bible study group. Purchase a Bible devotional. Create a prayer list. The list of ways to spend time with God goes on and on. Whichever method you decide, "stay focused."

Although there are many methods for spending time with God, the key here is to develop your own relationship with the Lord. Your time with God will not look like everyone else's. For example, I am married to a wonderful man. Our relationship is specific to us. There are couples that we hang out with, and their marriages are totally different from ours. In some cases, how they handle certain things in their relationship is totally opposite of how my husband and I would do it.

It is the same with your relationship with God. Your

time with God is personal. So don't compare it to anyone else's. Don't mimic anyone else. You can get pointers from them, but definitely make your relationship your own.

As I write this, another example comes to mind. When you get a new house, there is such excitement about how to decorate it. Think of your time with God as you and Him picking out furnishings to make your house a home.

Don't focus on feelings because, over time, your feelings will change. Sometimes you will feel tired, sleepy, hurt, angry, sensitive, etc. However, you will always feel safe and at home when you spend time with God.

Life Lesson

Time with God is just that—time spent with Him. Although we should allot a specific time to talk to Him daily, we should be keenly aware of His presence wherever we are. We're told in the latter part of Matthew 28:20: "Lo, I am with you always, even til the end of the earth." The Lord is always with us. So, we should acknowledge Him in all our ways so that He can direct our steps.

Time for You

Being a military spouse has afforded me lots of opportunities to travel. I have been to several different countries and various cities throughout the United States. Most of these destinations are not within walking distance. Therefore, I have traveled on planes to get there.

During the safety brief on each flight, the travelers are

given instructions in the event of a sudden drop in cabin pressure. We're informed that masks will fall from the overhead compartment. If traveling with small children, the adult traveler is directed to secure their mask and then assist the minor. I find it quite interesting that the airline's focus is on self-preservation. They realize that if you put yourself first, you are able to help someone else. These are my sentiments, exactly.

You are no good to anyone else unless you are good to yourself. We have been subconsciously duped by thinking (either self-inflicted or we're brainwashed) that we are being selfish if we think of ourselves first. Taking care of yourself is not selfish; it is self-care. Most of us have not been taught how to take care of ourselves. Rather, we have been taught how to take care of others.

I am not trying to offend anyone by saying this, but I was raised in the South. Our history as descendants of slaves has been to put the needs of others before our own. This train of thought has been passed down through our generations. However, I am adamant about making sure everyone who enters my sphere of influence gets the message that it's okay to love yourself.

Now, I'm not referring to becoming arrogant and self-absorbed. I'm conveying that you shouldn't feel condemned when you decide to show yourself some love. For example, You should enjoy those moments when making a big purchase for yourself, wearing a new outfit, or living in a nice home. I still find myself at times "dumbing" down compliments, as if I don't deserve them. However, when I catch myself doing that, I quickly self-correct. God's will is that we take proper care of ourselves.

What? know ye not that your body is the temple
of the Holy Ghost which is in you, which ye have
of God and you are not your own.

1 Corinthians 6:19

Your body is not your property. It was given to you by
God. So, take care of yourself just as any good renter would
maintain the property of the landlord.

Taking care of yourself does not always have to involve
money. I know you have heard the saying, "Some of the
best things in life are free," and this is true. So, take a walk
on the beach. Hold your loved one's hand. Create an altar
or space for prayer. Throw a rock, or just look up at the
stars. Be intentional about keeping your peace. Laugh out
loud, even if nothing is funny.

There are enough things in life that will make you
sad or give you the blues. Change your thoughts as if you
were choosing a different song on your playlist. Do what
it takes to maintain your mental health. If you need to see
a therapist, do that. If you need to talk to someone, find
a trustworthy person who loves the Lord to help you find
some direction in life. By all means, pray. Ask God, and He
will direct your steps.

Life Lesson

*I hope you are getting the lesson I am trying
to convey. You are important. You matter. You
are valuable, even if someone doesn't think so.
Sometimes for good reasons and sometimes for
not-so-good reasons, you will be despised, just as
it was with Jesus. However, that person or persons*

can't add to or take away from your value. The only One who was eligible to purchase your life was God. He sent His Son from heaven to do it. So, lift your head up. Walk with a little pep in your step. Take the time needed to maintain the wonderful creation God made. That creation is "you." Make a space for you.

Time for Others

God said to Jesus, "Son, I need for You to take a trip to earth and redeem My people by way of crucifixion." Now, we may never know the exact dialogue between the Godhead. However, we know that Jesus was willing to participate.

Jesus came to earth to die for people—billions upon billions of people. Just think about it. That kind of love for mankind is inexplicable. God saw us in our sinful, messed-up state and decided He needed to send Jesus to save us. God saw us and took time to make a plan, resulting in our salvation. In addition, Jesus made a space in time to carry out the plan. As you know, He put on a robe of flesh and became one of us.

Isaiah 53:5-8 in the New King James Version says:

But he was wounded for our transgressions, he was bruised for our iniquities: the chastisement of our peace was upon him; and with his stripes we are healed. All we like sheep have gone astray; we have turned every one to his own way; and the Lord hath laid on him the iniquity of us all. He was oppressed, and he was afflicted, yet he opened not his mouth: he is brought as a lamb to the slaughter, and as a sheep before her shearers is dumb, so he openeth not his mouth. He was taken from prison and from judgment: and who shall declare his generation? for he was cut off out of the land of the living: for the transgression of my people was he stricken.

Wow, my heart is touched just thinking about the previous scriptures. We meant so much to the Lord that He would humble Himself in such a way to rescue us. He set an example for how we should treat others. Of course, we cannot do what only He could, but we can make time for each other. We can treat people the way we would like to be treated. We can have a mind like His to focus on the needs of others.

You may think no one needs you, but trust me, someone does. Our pastor says, "You may not be for everybody, but you are for somebody." Someone needs your warmth, your smile, and your words of wisdom. There are people who need food, shelter, and clothing. The elderly among us need you to slow down and make them feel seen. Our youngsters need to know how you made it through the rough spots in life. Our girls need to know how to be women. Our boys need to know how to be men. Ask God to show you who needs your God-given gifts. Then, make the deposits into their lives. This is creating space for others.

A good teacher realizes the best students may not always sit at the front of the classroom. That is why the teacher is trained to reach the front, middle, and back of the class. The goal is that no one is left behind.

Realistically, some children fall through the cracks.

However, in the school of life, we must do our part. So, show the love of God to whoever will receive it. We need to make time for each other. We never know when or if we will get to see certain people again.

Life Lesson

It is so easy to get caught up in the everyday matters of life. Work, school, church, television, and cell phones all have their part in absorbing time in our lives. While these things are good, we must remember to maintain a balance in order to avoid burnout. Above all else, value the essentials of carving out space for God, yourself, and others.

78

Chapter 8

Say Yes or No

But let your communication be, Yea, Yea: Nay,
Nay for whatsoever is more than these cometh
of evil.

Matthew 5:37

This chapter is not for the faint of heart. You must develop a
certain amount of courage to let your yes be yes and your no
be no. The aforementioned Bible passage is simply telling
us to be people of integrity. Therefore, our word should
stand on its own.

Have you ever been around a person who is habitually
indecisive? How about someone who dramatizes or over
embellishes when it comes to answering questions? After a
while, you don't believe anything they say. I mean, you ask
them a question that requires a yes or no answer, and they
give you everything but a direct answer.

Jesus conveyed that when we exaggerate things, there
is an evil presence in the midst. Little kids exemplify how
this scripture should be displayed in our lives. For instance,
Johnny has a piece of candy, and you ask, "Johnny, can I
have some of your candy?" Johnny's answer is an emphatic
"yes" or an outright "no." He did not beat around the bush
or get your hopes up with flowery terminology. It was a

simple "yes" or "no."

It is important to possess the fortitude to say "yes" or "no." The decision is totally yours. I am not saying you should not seek the advice of others or compile whatever data is needed to help you make your decision. By all means, consult with others and do the research, but at the end of the day, you must make your own decisions. Then, stand behind them.

Embrace the Conflict

Nobody likes being the "bad guy." I get it; it is easier to go along and get along. How many times have we said "yes" when we really meant "no?" This is a struggle for many people because we want to fit in with our peers. Saying "no" can create conflicts. For people who do not like confrontation, it can be an uncomfortable situation. In many cases, saying "no" breeds uncertainty about the future. We wonder if the other party will still like us. Will they dissociate themselves from us?

Mark Gorkin, MSW, LICSW, "The Stress Doc" ™, a licensed clinical social worker, said, "A firm no a day keeps the ulcers away, and hostilities, too." I totally agree with him. I wanted to talk about this because it is frustrating to do things you oppose. Stay focused; hear me out. Doing things you may not want to do is part of life. For instance, you must work in order to provide for your family. You may not want to work, but you say "yes" to work and the things that come along with it. You may dislike cleaning your house. Yet, when you consider the long-term effects of a dirty environment, you clean to alleviate the problem.

Nevertheless, these are not the instances I'm referring to. I am talking about random requests from people that you don't want to perform. For instance, your very best and highly regarded friend asks you to go hiking on your day off. You really, really, really don't want to go because you marked this day on your calendar as time for household chores. You also wanted to finish a book you started reading. Subsequently, you fear saying "no" because it will hurt their feelings. In this case, you should say "no." Unless your friend is depressed or has some other extenuating circumstance that requires your immediate attention, your answer should be a resounding "no." And don't feel bad about it. A mature person will understand and back off. On the other hand, a selfish individual will keep prodding and pulling until they get their way.

Most often, we say "yes" at the expense of our own self-care. What is self-care, you may ask? Let's sit with this for a moment. I was reading an article entitled "What is Self-Care and Why is It Important?" I received a wealth of knowledge.

I learned that self-care can be divided into several parts. The parts are emotional, mental, physical, social, and spiritual. First, let's talk about emotional care. This can be accomplished by taking time to relax and doing things you enjoy. The emphasis here is on what you—yes, you—enjoy. What you like matters. It should matter to your friends and family as well. Most importantly, it should matter to you.

Whether reading a book, catching a movie, decorating, sewing, etc., it all matters. In addition, emotional self-care is the ability to say "no" to unwanted activities, as we mentioned above. Trust me, it is liberating to loosen yourself from the bondage of saying "yes" to everything and everyone all the time. I firmly believe agreeing with everything is deeply rooted in "people pleasing." You will never please everyone. So, get over that notion and say "yes" when you mean yes and "no" when you mean no.

Life Lesson

My dad used to say, "Your word is your bond." It was his way of saying that if I tell you I am going to do something, you can count on it, and vice versa. I have learned that people respect you more when you are able to stand by your sound, well-thought-out decisions.

Then there is mental self-care. This means taking it easy and not being so hard on yourself. Sometimes, we are our own worst critics. It is imperative that we change that narrative. We tend to feel guilty if we have to present an opposing view to an argument. Although you didn't initiate the argument, your opinion was sought. Therefore, you gave your perspective. As a result, you may feel mental stress.

In certain situations, saying "no" to others can be as difficult as saying "yes." Trust me, you will feel the mental weight of it, especially if your "no or yes" faces opposition. It is important to stand firm during those times because this is pivotal to preserving your mental well-being. Train your brain to accept opposition. It is not the end of the world if your decision is not well received. I have learned that being liked by everyone is overrated. You'll sleep better at night knowing you have done the right thing.

Next, we must care for ourselves physically. To me, this

is the most challenging of them all. I am not a big fan of exercise, but it is necessary. I tell myself "no" to exercising all the time …lol. However, it is important. So, I force myself into the gym to improve physically. My husband has taught me a neat trick. It seems to work. He helped me make a playlist on my phone that consists of about six songs, about four to five minutes in length. While listening to my playlist, I do circuit training on the few pieces of gym equipment we have in our home. Every time a song on my playlist comes to an end, I go to a different machine. Needless to say, I am saying "no" to what I want and "yes" to what I need. My body thanks me for it. Well, I certainly hope it does.

Social self-care is needed as well. We need to get out and meet people. Making friends and attending social events can be fun. It is important that we connect, either in person or using social media. God doesn't want us to isolate ourselves. I have been in that place before. I can tell you firsthand: be intentional about this type of self-care because you can become content just by being in your own world.

Realize that there is someone who needs your conversation, your creativity, etc. And you need theirs. In the world we live in, we need each other to survive. Thus, it is important to have meaningful friendships and be in a space where you can let your hair down.

I have a group of friends. We laugh, we cry, and we pray for each other. It is a wonderful thing. I think the beauty of our friendships is that we also give each other space. I didn't have these types of relationships with people earlier in my life. Even still, God knew what was best for me, and I have moved on. It is important to have friends that respect your "no" as well as your "yes." They are what I like to call "forever friends."

Finally, spiritual self-care is a must. The source of this self-maintenance is my faith in Jesus Christ. Everyone reading this book may not believe the way I do, and that is okay. You have the right to choose. However, for me, my faith is everything. It is the very foundation of my well-being.

God, in the person of Jesus Christ, saved my natural and spiritual lives. He delivered me from dangers seen and unseen. The Lord made me free from the laws of sin and death. I will be forever grateful for the sacrifice He made for me on the cross of Calvary. God gave me peace on the inside.

Nowadays, you don't see a lot of people enjoying inner peace. There is so much mental anguish and anxiety in our world. So, I feel it's necessary to get around people who love the Lord and are grounded in Him. Go to church, read the Bible, be filled with the Holy Spirit (Acts 2:38), and pray. These spiritual practices have helped my life tremendously. They keep me at peace when everything around me is in an uproar. Don't get me wrong, I have experienced some very low points in my life. However, my friend Jesus sticks closer than any brother. He has given me firm footing on some very shaky ground.

Benefits of solitude

I mentioned earlier that making an unpopular decision will have consequences. Yet don't allow that to become your focus. When Jesus told us to let our "yes" be yes and our "no" be no, I believe He wanted us to be honest and upright. Jesus is the perfect example. He faced so much opposition. Yet He did not compromise on His decisions.

Our Lord felt the wrath of the Jews and the Roman soldiers. Simultaneously, He felt the peace of God. When you are completely honest with yourself and others, you benefit from peace. Sometimes Jesus walked with crowds and sometimes with a few loyal followers. However, most of the time, He walked alone. Overall, we should make decisions that please God and bring us joy and inner peace.

Life Lesson

The pleasure of pleasing people only lasts for a moment, but the benefits of pleasing God will last from now until eternity.

CHAPTER 9

God Heals Wounds

But He was wounded for our transgression, he was bruised for our iniquities: the chastisement of our peace was upon him; and with his stripes we are healed.

Isaiah 53:5

Have you ever been in pain? At the time of this writing, there are about 8 billion people in the world. I guarantee you that at some point in time, they all experienced some kind of pain. We have all been dealt a proverbial hand to play one of the cards in the deck—pain.

Pain comes in many forms. It comes packaged as physical, sensory, behavioral, sociocultural, cognitive, affective, or spiritual. I can't speak for you, but as for me, I don't like pain in any form. I think the most excruciating pain I have ever felt is that of childbirth. Oh, my goodness. Although there was pain, a beautiful blessing came out of it. This may have been one of my first realizations that pain can be good and bad at the same time.

God did not promise us we would live free from trouble.

So, let us not accuse Him falsely when we go through things. He's the same in good and bad times. The issue is not that we will experience some sort of pain; it's how we handle the pain.

The depths of pain can leave you speechless or force you to scream. Yet, it is a tool that teaches some of the most important lessons in life. For instance, I learned very early in life not to touch a hot stove because it would burn you. When it comes to pain, discernment is critical. You need the ability to see trouble from afar to avoid entangling yourself in painful situations.

In addition, I have encountered the pain of rejection. It taught me I am not for everyone, and everyone is not for me. That's okay. The pain of loneliness has shown me my one true friend—Jesus. When no one else shows up for me, He never fails. He will show up every time. Sometimes we can become so emotional when people let us down. However, don't get mad or upset. We live among human beings with limited abilities. Albeit, God is able to be everywhere at once.

Then there's the pain from jealousy. Some people are not happy with the gift of life. They are not happy with themselves and blame you. They perceive your life as perfect. Life is far from perfect. I have been a victim of poverty. The pain of this experience taught me to appreciate what I have and to be thankful for all the blessings God bestows in my life.

Being mistreated has taught me to treat others as I want to be treated. Being betrayed has taught me to appreciate good friends and to be loyal. The pain of being shunned because of my race has taught me to appreciate and respect diversity. The pain of being a woman has taught me to love hard and be true to myself. The list goes on and on.

There are pains that come with every aspect of life. For instance, there is the pain of motherhood. Now, I'm not merely speaking of labor and delivery. I'm talking about the pain that comes along with raising children. Other painstaking obligations could come from being a spouse, sibling, or friend. There's also pain in employment as well as in organized religion. No one is exempt. Even Jesus had to endure the pain of being the Savior of the world.

Earlier, I mentioned a few types of pain. Let's take a few moments to discuss them. Google defines physical pain as an unpleasant feeling, such as a prick, tingle, sting, burn, or ache. Pain may be sharp or dull. It may come and go, or it may be constant. You may feel pain in one area of your body, such as your back, abdomen, chest, or pelvis, or you may feel pain all over.

Pain can be helpful in diagnosing a problem. If you have ever gone to the doctor, they will ask if you are feeling any pain. Then they ask for the pain's location. Medication is administered for pain to help bring healing to your body. In some instances, they will ask you to analyze your pain on a scale of one to ten. This lets me know that you can live with some level of pain.

There is sensory pain. This kind of pain involves hearing, smell, taste, touch, and vision. Writing about this category of pain really illuminated what Jesus must have gone through on the cross. Can you imagine Him hearing all the snide remarks of His critics? He tasted the bitter mixture they gave Him to quench His thirst. He felt the piercing thrash of the cat-of-nine-tails as it ripped His flesh. Finally, He saw the hate in the face of His enemies. This had to be a painful experience. Just think: He subjected Himself to excruciating pain in order to heal our pain.

Next is sociocultural pain, which is an emotional and behavioral response based on an individual's past experiences and perceptions of pain. This type of pain is one I know quite well. This kind of pain can trigger bad behavior, which leads to bad decisions. Sociocultural pain causes a lot of regret.

There are some things I have done that I wish I could take back. When I think of them, it causes my heart to ache, and I yearn for an eraser. You and I both know we cannot undo the wrongs we have done to others or the wrongs that have been committed against us. Hence, I am so thankful for the cross of Christ. He has forgiven every sin and paid for all my wrongs with His blood. My past is behind me, and a bright future awaits me. I now live free of the pain of guilt and shame, and it is all because of Jesus. He healed my pain and continues to do so.

Be mindful of how you process painful situations in life. Hence, cognitive pain. We are all susceptible to being hurt. So, let's get a jump on it by compiling a strategy for how we handle it when it happens. Prayer should be at the top of that list. Talking to God brings unexplainable peace when you are hurting. In addition, talk to someone who has your best interests at heart and will tell you the truth.

Going to therapy is a viable option. Therapists are trained to deal with all kinds of pain. My point is that we can't do it alone. No one is an island. People need people.

Another kind of pain is affective pain. This speaks to the frustration of painful situations and can lead to depression and anger. Then, lastly, spiritual pain occurs when we perceive that godly principles or morals are being violated. I don't know about you, but I do not like to feel like I am displeasing God in some way.

I am so glad I have learned the Lord loves me just the way I am. He is not waiting somewhere in the background to make my life miserable with guilt. Now, I am not saying God has given me a free pass to sin—nope, not by any means. Nevertheless, the Lord has made it clear that He loves me through good and bad. God receives me just as the father did for the prodigal son. God is in the restoration business, not the demolition business.

At some point, for all of us, pain is inevitable. However, we don't have to succumb to pain because it doesn't always last. God sent His only Son to earth to deliver us from the ultimate pain (the sting and penalty of sin). He saw our condition and created a remedy. God wants us healed, whole, and blessed.

I will leave you with this story about my grandson. He loves baseball. When I say he loves baseball, I mean he really loves it. He is going to try out for the team again this year. He tried out last year and didn't make it. Not making the team was a very painful experience for him.

Well, the other day, he told me he was really nervous about the tryouts. As his Nana, I wanted this to happen for him. However, I told him to remain in a good place mentally and emotionally, whether he's on the team or not. Do you know what I was teaching him? I was teaching him how to handle the pain.

Again, I hope he makes the team. However, I know that in life, making the team is not a guarantee. After all, my grandson eventually got over the pain of not making the team last year. So he set his sights on playing the drums.

We must first make the choice to move on. Don't throw a pity party and sit and sulk over the loss. The lesson is that God heals us from our pain if we will allow Him. There is a lot of life to experience.

Life Lesson

Let God heal you everywhere you hurt so you can walk in the destiny God has planned for you.

Chapter 10

The Greatest Life Lesson

Get Jesus

After reading the previous chapters, I am sure you have concluded that I love God and appreciate the gift He has given us in His Son, Jesus Christ. Yes, I am a believer. We are born in sin and shaped in iniquity because Adam and Eve broke the covenant between God and man in the Garden of Eden. From that point on, their sin was passed on from generation to generation.

> For God so loved the world that He gave His only begotten Son, that whosoever believeth in him should not perish but have everlasting life.
>
> *John 3:16*

I believe that Jesus was born to a virgin named Mary. Jesus was God clothed in humanity, walking the earth. At the appointed time, He submitted Himself to the humiliation of a bloody cross to restore our divine connection to the Father. This single act broke the curse of *spiritual death* that we inherited from Adam and Eve. Three days later, Jesus rose from the dead with power over death, hell and the grave.

In addition to that, I believe in the love of God. He loves us and wants what is best for us. He is a gentleman and will not force His way into our lives. Like anyone, He wants to be chosen. Please choose Him today because He has already chosen you.

If you have decided to choose Him today, please pray this prayer with me.

Prayer of Salvation

Father, Your Word says in Romans 10:9-10 that if I confess with my mouth that Jesus is Lord and believe in my heart that You raised Him from the dead, I will be saved. So, right now, forgive me for every sin I have committed against You, knowingly and unknowingly. I confess that Jesus is my Lord and choose Him as Lord of my life right now. I believe in my heart that You raised Him from the dead. I put away my past life of sin and shame. I close the door to all of the devil's devices. I am a new spiritual creation because Jesus is my Lord and Saviour. Old things have passed away, and all things have become new in Jesus' name, Amen.

Congratulations, you are a Christian, "a follower of Christ." Does this mean that all of your problems will go away? Not necessarily. However, it does mean that if you acknowledge God in all your ways, He will direct your path. It means if you should die today, you have a home in heaven. Be confident that when you are absent from this natural body, you are present with the Lord (2 Corinthians 5:8). These are just a few benefits.

I encourage you to study the Bible, and learn about Him for yourself. It is good to hear about Him from others, but you will get the most out of the relationship when you know Him for yourself. Ask Him to direct your path to a church that is right for you. Every Christian needs a Pastor, for Jeremiah 3:15 says, "And I will give you pastors according to mine heart, which shall feed you with knowledge and understanding."

Please note that Churches are filled with "infallible" beings called "humans." There is no perfect person, so there is no perfect church. However, we are strengthened by each other. Jesus is coming back for His bride, the church. God is with us, and we will not fail.

Final Thoughts

In conclusion, there is no way I can cram every lesson I have learned into these few pages. However, I hope you will appreciate the ones I have shared. Knowing that I have motivated you to fulfill your God-given purpose would be a blessing. Please be fully aware that you were born with intentionality and purpose.

You may become a prolific speaker or professional athlete, sing in Carnegie Hall, or your name may never be in the spotlight. Only God knows. Either way, I want you to know that you are valuable. You are unique; God created you with His artistic hands. You are the original, and there is no duplicate copy. You are a reflection of Christ. So, cherish that person you see in the mirror every day. You are God's creation. Therefore, allow His light to shine through you.

I hope you will love your family. Love them hard, flaws and all. They are not perfect, but God chose them for your life. Give them their flowers while they live. Tomorrow is not promised to any of us. So, be grateful and thankful for every day you spend with them. Once they are gone, you can't turn the clock back.

Love your family in such a way that there will be no regrets. Loving them will sometimes mean you have to say the hard things. There is a misconception about love. Some believe love doesn't rock the boat or cause conflict. I am here to tell you that sometimes both are necessary, especially with those you love. Your love for them will cause you to say things to them that others will not say. On occasion, love pushes and confronts.

Love means standing with them when the world has turned its back on them. There are three words everyone in your family should hear: "I love you." If I could add a fourth word, it would be "unconditionally." This does not mean you condone bad behavior. It simply means what it means. It is what God continually does for us. Love your family like He loves us. God has given us a promise in His word: Love never fails (1 Cor 13:8)

I challenge you to be your authentic self. There is no need to put on airs or impress anyone. God knows the real you, and anything else you try to portray is counterfeit. If you see beauty in your life, you won't be jealous of others. Once you learn to appreciate yourself, don't become arrogant. You are free to be confident.

Let your thoughts, words and actions line up with your life. Be mindful not to be manipulated by peer pressure. Don't lose yourself under the influence of others. Prayerfully, make your own decisions. You are not responsible for how people respond to your authenticity, but be authentic, anyway. People may not like you. In fact, they may shun and judge you. However, they will respect your authenticity at the end of the day.

You're not the only one on this journey. You will meet so many people along the way. There are good and bad people. I pray that you will be able to discern the people who have been placed there by God and those who have been sent by the wicked one. So don't go through life with blinders on.

There is a real God who loves you and wants the best for you; the people who love Him will want the same. While this is true, you must also know that a real enemy hates good, and his followers have the same mindset.

Therefore, you must be wise in choosing your circle of acquaintances. Every encounter is valuable, and you will learn something from each experience. Keep a clear head. Don't become addicted to things that will alter your thinking—drugs, alcohol, smoking, etc—as well as your mental state. As a result, they can leave you unable to make sound decisions. This is one way the devil captures souls for his kingdom.

Stay alert. Be vigilant because the Bible tells us our adversary, the devil, goes about as a roaring lion, seeking whom he may devour (1 Pet 5:8). I can't stress this enough: you should get Christ and keep Him at the forefront of your life. He is the anchor that will keep you firm and steady as you navigate life's twists and turns.

Jesus will never leave or forsake you. Still, you must make space for Him (Isa 26:3). Be mindful: everyone deserves to be respected, loved and supported. The Bible records, "Here is a simple, rule-of-thumb guide for behavior: Ask yourself what you want people to do for you, then grab the initiative and do it for them" (Mat 7:12 MSG). So, be responsible, honest, hardworking, firm, fair, loving, kind, strong, God-fearing, decisive, and most importantly, an obedient child of God.

As I conclude this book, I love sharing the lessons I have learned to help others on their journey. I hope you will feel the same way. One of my purposes is to share this legacy of my life lessons with you. Now, pay it forward. Let's leave this world better than we found it.

My Life Lessons

Meet the Author

Precedere A. Wilson is from Kinston, North Carolina. She graduated from the University of Phoenix, Phoenix, Arizona, with a Bachelor's degree in Business Management in 2015. She obtained an Associate degree in Accounting with a minor in Business in 1994 from Sullivan University, Louisville, Kentucky. She earned a level II Department of Defense Financial Management Certification in 2015 and obtained a Ministerial Certification from Sonship School of the Firstborn in 2010.

She works as an Accountant for the National Training Center, Ft Irwin, California, and serves with her husband as a congregational Elder at Destiny Christian Center, Victorville, California. She and her husband have been married for 35 years and have traveled many places spreading the gospel of Jesus Christ.

She has two adult children, a son-in-law and two beautiful grandchildren. Her hobbies include reading, writing, sewing and adding value to people. Her motto is and always will be, "Leave people and places better than you found them."

For Speaking Inquiries:

PrecedereAWilson@gmail.com

 Ann Wilson

 Zedetae00